MW00612165

The
Tireless Teacher
Toolkit

The Tireless Teacher Toolkit

51 MINI LESSONS for LANGUAGE ARTS TEACHERS to Keep Students READING, WRITING, LISTENING, and SPEAKING Until THE BELL RINGS

ROSEANNE CHENG

WISE Ink
CREATIVE ★ PUBLISHING

ISBN: 978-1-63489-242-1
Library of Congress Catalog Number: 2019940777
Printed in the United States of America
First Printing: 2019
23 22 21 20 19   5 4 3 2 1

Book design by Athena Currier

Wise Ink Creative Publishing.
807 Broadway Street NE, Suite 46
Minneapolis, MN 55413
wiseink.com

To all the educators who have paved my way,
and to all the teachers in the trenches.

CONTENTS

INTRODUCTION

Hi! If you have purchased this book, you fall into one of several categories:

YOU ARE A BRAND-NEW TEACHER. Ah, I remember those days. You're done writing papers, reading about pedagogy, observing, and stressing about finding a job, and now you are gainfully employed by a school district. Maybe it's August, and your first in-service day is coming up next week. And you're thinking to yourself, "Um, holy sh*t. I am going to be teaching in a few weeks and I have no idea what to do."

If this describes you, then welcome to the wonderful world of teaching. August panic is totally normal, as are November doldrums and May crazies. This book will be an awesome resource for you as you navigate this new world.

YOU KNOW AND LOVE A TEACHER. You might not be a teacher your-self, but you understand that teaching is no joke. Maybe your child is just embarking on a career in teaching, or maybe a huge group of college friends has just received their licenses and you want to give them a little something to help them along their journey.

If this describes you, God bless you. I mean it. Lots of people pay lip service to how much they appreciate teachers, but when it comes to actually supporting them with anything tangible, they are MIA. This book is a great gift for the teachers in your life, so thank you for giving it.

YOU ARE A VETERAN TEACHER LOOKING FOR NEW IDEAS. Teaching can be an isolating job, and an easy way to burn out is to do the same things over and over with no change. Maybe you are just look-ing for ways to build upon the toolkit you've already created. Maybe you've reflected on the last several years of teaching and realized you've had more than a handful of days when a book like this would have made a difference for you.

If this describes you, I offer a huge hug and a handshake for your service to your community. I'm happy you've picked up this book. There will be ideas in here that will reinvigorate you and your career and remind you why you got into this awe-some profession in the first place.

YOU TEACH TEACHERS. Is there anything more exciting than teaching people who want to learn? No. And maybe that is why you've picked up this book. Maybe you are looking to create a list of resources for your students to use as they study the craft. Maybe you've been stuck when your students have asked you how to fill small bits of time in the classroom. Maybe you just want to give your students a little something tangible for when the first bell rings and teaching life gets real.

If this describes you, thank you for your purchase and thank you for taking the time to inspire another generation of teachers. We need you!

A little about me before we get started.

I began my teaching career in 2005, after four years working in high tech. It's a long story. Actually, no it's not. Despite making great money in the business world, I was twenty-five years old and absolutely miserable in my job. You know that line in the movie *Office Space*, where Peter tells his therapist that every day he walks into his office is the worst day of his life? It was like that.

Then I got a role at the company training new hires, and guess what I discovered? I am a great teacher. I loved breaking things down so people could understand them, I loved fielding thoughtful questions, and I *loved* creating curriculums. So I figured it was time to go back to school, get my teaching degree, and teach high school English.

My first teaching gig was as a student teacher/intern in an affluent Silicon Valley suburb. My next teaching gig was a three-year stint at a private international school in Beijing. After that, I went back to Silicon Valley to teach at an urban public school, and then to Minnesota, where I taught a huge, largely rural student population. Then I wrote a couple young adult novels and moved into the publishing world, and I continue teaching creative writing workshops in the Minneapolis area.

I've never been tenured in a district because I have moved around a ton. I see this as a huge advantage. I've seen a lot of the world and taught in vastly different environments. I know alllllll kinds of kids. But no matter what school (or country) I was teaching in, I learned this above all else:

A teacher's time in the classroom is their number-one resource. A teacher who cannot manage their time well will struggle day in and day out.

Even the best teachers struggle with time management, oftentimes through no fault of their own. Sometimes the most thoughtfully planned-out lessons simply go faster than the teacher anticipated. Sometimes an unexpected fire drill interrupts the students' workflow and sends a lesson off course. Sometimes teachers have one prep with fifteen students and another with thirty, which dramatically impacts the length of a lesson. Sometimes there's something happening in the news that day that causes everyone to be distracted. Sometimes teachers just look out at the sea of faces before them in the classroom and realize that the kids are simply not paying attention anymore.

Oh, and that doesn't even take into consideration that teachers are, in fact, human. (Shocking, I know!) Sometimes they don't sleep well. Sometimes they're distracted by events in their personal lives. Sometimes, like all humans, they forget things.

All teachers have been there. Many times. In fact, it's probably more accurate to say that this happens constantly. If I had a quarter for every time I looked up at the clock in my classroom and realized I had fifteen minutes left until the bell rang and no idea how I should best use that time, I could probably buy myself a round-trip ticket somewhere tropical.

In those moments, teachers have a choice. They can throw their hands up and give kids fifteen minutes to chat with each other, catch up on other work (valuable, sometimes), or put their heads down to take a quick catnap (not recommended)—or they can use those moments to teach something. Not something that the kids will be tested on. But something valuable just the same.

That is why I created this book. To help teachers maximize *this* time in the classroom, these extra fifteen minutes in which, even though your best-laid plans have gone awry, you're still a kick-ass teacher anyway.

HOW TO USE THIS BOOK:

DISCLAIMER: This book is a handy-dandy resource. That is it. It is not meant to take the place of detailed, standards-based unit planning. It is not meant to be used for summative or formative assessments. It's not meant to be attached to any set of state standards, college prep course, or particular book or lesson plan.

Please, no rubrics.

While none of the lessons in here are meant to take up an entire class period, this doesn't mean that they couldn't be created to do so. Lots of the ideas in here could be more thoroughly applied to the standards for your classroom. You know yourself and your kids best. If you are inspired, build upon the lessons! And then tweet me a picture of your awesomeness.

There is going to be some up-front work you'll have to do to build your toolkit. For now, I want you to start thinking of yourself as a collector. You know those teachers who have stacks of yellowed newspapers in the back of their classrooms that no one uses? *That is not what I mean.* Think of yourself as a careful curator of information and resources for your *Oh, sh*t—we still have fifteen minutes* toolkit. Once you're in the habit of collecting great stuff, you'll find that it's easy and not at all time-consuming. It's just part of who you are.

A note about technology: I love technology. Technology is great. But I have found that technology in the classroom should be carefully thought out and planned. This book is for those "Oh sh*t" moments when you realize you have some time to fill in a meaningful way. Fiddling with your computer, overhead projector, or sound system is a great way to waste a ton of time. So this book is filled with lessons that you would do, in theory, sans technology.

Quite a few of these lessons require students to take out their cell phones and research quickly. Here's the deal: We live in an age where most kids have smartphones (therefore, tons of information) at their fingertips. I, along with many of you, have a love-hate relationship with this device. What I found during my years in the classroom was that I could either spend a ton of time keeping kids from looking at

their phones (I was never successful) or I could embrace it and use the darn things to my advantage. Every teacher is different on this. So if there is a lesson idea in here that you don't want kids whipping their phones out for, then you absolutely should make that call. But keep alternate sources for reference handy.

Again, if you decide to build upon any of these lessons and incorporate technology, go right ahead. Similarly, if you can't stand the thought of recycling all that scratch paper and your students have laptops anyway, you absolutely should have them do the lessons that require writing on Google Docs or whatever else it is you use. Totally cool.

I suggest keeping this book (and the toolkit you create for it) in a place that is easily accessible to you. Don't put together a box of crap that goes on top of your bookcase where you can't reach it. Again, this is a quick reference. Time is of the essence. You don't want to waste a bunch of it sorting through dusty papers.

Have mercy on your poor substitute teachers: provide them a copy of this book and show them where your toolkit is in your classroom. You and I both know that your sub plans are precarious at best, and no one deserves a break more than an overworked, underappreciated sub.

Lastly, you'll notice that I leave some note-taking space next to each activity. This is intentional. Remember all those hours in teacher credential classes when your teachers talked about the importance of reflection? And how you totally know how important it is, but you definitely don't have time to do it regularly?

Consider that blank space your "reflection" place. No full sentences allowed. Just make a note about what did and didn't work when you did the activity in your classroom so you know for next year. I recommend writing in pencil so you can erase, rethink, and try again.

Got it? I think we're set.

THE TIRELESS TEACHER

TOOLKIT

Pardon my French, but the realization that you have fifteen more minutes of class and nothing meaningful to do with that time is often followed by the phrase, "Oh sh*t." It just is. Fine, maybe you say shoot. I don't.

Teachers use the word "toolkit" loosely. For some teachers, Pinterest is their "toolkit." Maybe they have a list of websites they go to for inspiration and call *that* their toolkit. Maybe they have a binder of torn-out lesson plans they've gotten from other teachers over the years, thinking they'll get to them on a rainy day.

Here's the problem with those types of toolkits: they take too much time to access. Once you've glanced up at that clock and your kids sense you're a little panicked at the thought of filling time, you've lost them. There is no reality where your students

11

will allow you to leisurely scroll through a couple websites while you figure out something to do with them. (You wish!)

You need to have something *at the ready*. And that is what this toolkit is all about.

Here is a list of ideas for your toolkit. I don't care how you organize or store it, as long as it's accessible to you. I suggest grabbing a few bookshelves from some forgotten corner of the school (or your local Goodwill), along with some big plastic bins. Oh, and maintaining the toolkit is easy. If you have a teacher assistant (TA) or a parent helper, there is plenty in here for them to organize or collect on your behalf. Also, if you have a student staying after class for less-than-stellar behavior, there's a lot here they can do for you too. But truthfully, once you are on the lookout for these items and make collecting them and maintaining them a part of your routine, it's easy.

- **COLLECT GREAT MAGAZINES.** You don't need a lot. A stack of ten to twenty is great. Choose carefully: *Newsweek*, *Time*, the *New Yorker*, things like that. You know your students' reading level. If you have a TA, you can have them cut out short and appropriate articles and store them in a folder.

- **COLLECT *SOME* NEWSPAPER ARTICLES.** Notice I did not say to collect stacks and stacks of newspapers. Just some interesting articles. Keep an eye out, and have friends keep an eye out too. Once you have a stack of twenty to thirty, you probably have enough for your toolkit. You can always add, purge, or swap. Make sure you are only saving the articles you want to use—not the entire newspaper.

- **HAVE A GALLON ZIPLOCK BAG OF TRINKETS.** No need to fill it to the brim. Feathers, rocks, small toys, coins, old keys, etc. You can use these things in many creative ways.

- **COLLECT POEMS.** Notice that I didn't say poetry anthologies, though you'll want those too. I'm talking about a stack of poems photocopied from books or printed from the internet. Don't worry if they're good, and don't worry if they're written by someone famous. Just collect a bunch.

- **COLLECT ANTHOLOGIES.** Goodwill is one of my favorite places to go for books, and not just for my own personal reading. Almost every time I go there, I find a short story or poetry anthology from someone's college days—a goldmine. The more diverse your collection, the better. You can rip great stories or poems out or keep them bound in the book—whatever works for you.

- **GET A CHEAP PAIR OF SPEAKERS TO PLUG INTO YOUR PHONE.** If you are gadgety, you might be tempted to get some fancy technology that hooks up to your interactive whiteboard and does all kinds of fancy sound stuff. That's not what I'm talking about. You should have speakers that you can decide to use and then use in a total of three seconds. Plug and play.

- **DOWNLOAD SOME AMAZING PODCASTS.** A few favorites: *Good Night Stories for Rebel Girls, Presidential, Hidden Brain, Constitutional, Invisibilia, Revisionist History, Story Pirates* (for young ones) . . . the list goes on and on. By the time you read this book, chances are there are many more to add to your podcast arsenal. You should always be on the lookout for recommendations.

- **COLLECT TED TALKS.** There are several websites with long lists of awesome TED talks for students. Growth mindset, organization, kindness, compassion—anything you can think of, it's on there. Have a few TED talks saved to your favorites at all times and pull them out when necessary.

- **THE *NEW YORK TIMES* (SPECIFICALLY, THE "LIVES" COLUMNS).** Sometimes your "Oh sh*t" moments will be so huge that none of the suggestions in this book will work, and your fifteen minutes needs to be story time. Here's the place for an awesome collection: www.nytimes.com/column/lives

- **COLLECT POSTCARDS.** Postcards are an awesome way to engage kids creatively, from writing stories to creating pictures and scenes.

- **COLLECT HOROSCOPES.** Horoscopes are creative writing gold.

- **INVEST IN A BOOK OF SIMPLE MONOLOGUES.** Make sure these are appropriate to the age group you teach. You will likely rip out the monologues so that you have a stack to pass out to students for your toolkit activities.

- **COLLECT OLD PICTURES.** Similar to postcards, old pictures can be a great way to inspire kids to think creatively. Having a stack of these in your toolkit is really fun.

- **COLLECT POCKET DICTIONARIES.** A class set would be ideal—ten to fifteen. (Yes, I know your class size is twice that. Kids can share.)

- **VISIT YOUR SCHOOL LIBRARIAN.** Ask them if there are any class sets of books—especially plays—that they simply don't use anymore. I did this once and found a class set of *The Merchant of Venice* that hadn't been opened since 1975. I brought them to my classroom, and voilà: toolkit gold.

- **COLLECT VOCABULARY WORDS.** Make a stack of index cards with super-challenging vocabulary words for your students. I'm talking SAT vocabulary words. Not the definitions, just the words. A recipe box or rubber band is great to store these.

- **COLLECT IDIOMATIC PHRASES.** Make a stack of index cards with idiomatic phrases on them. A cultural literacy anthology is a great place to start for this, or you can always consult the trusty internet. This is an easy job for your TA to do for you, if you have one.

- **COLLECT PHILOSOPHERS.** Maybe your collection is a stack of printed-out Wikipedia pages, or maybe it's pages you've ripped from a book. You could also just print out pictures from the internet. Either way, collect some simple bios of great thinkers to inspire your kids. You can use these in so many ways.

- **DOWNLOAD THE LIBBY APP.** Libby is life-changing for teachers. You load your library card information onto the app and borrow e-books and library books directly from there.

- COLLECT GREAT ARTISTIC IMAGES. These can be magazine clippings, small pieces of art, or cutouts from ads. If you have a coffee-table book collecting dust in your house, this is a great opportunity to cut out the images and actually use them.

- DOWNLOAD EPIC UNLIMITED BOOKS FOR KIDS. If you teach young kids, you might want to get this app and save yourself a ton of money on hardcover children's books!

- HAVE A STACK OF BINDER PAPER OR RECYCLED SCRAP PAPER. Because this is a toolkit, you're going to need the basics. Ever notice how long it takes for a student to rip a piece of paper out of their notebook? Or boot up their laptops? A stack of scratch paper is a basic necessity in your classroom. And speaking of the basics . . .

- HAVE A BAG OF PENCILS OR PENS TOO. Just because there is nothing more annoying than setting up an activity and hearing students grumble that they don't have a pencil.

- COLLECT PRIZES. None of the activities in this book are meant to be formally assessed, but that doesn't mean you shouldn't have prizes attached to them. I'm all about rewarding students with *something* to acknowledge that they've worked hard or taken a risk. A Hershey kiss is something. A silly temporary tattoo is something. A "gift certificate" for one extra minute on a timed test . . . *that's something*.

Still feeling overwhelmed? Or maybe like you've tapped into every toolkit option under the sun already? **OBSERVE TEACHERS OUTSIDE YOUR DISCIPLINE.** What can an English teacher learn from a biology teacher? Turns out *a whole lot*. Observing other teachers in action is one of the best ways to figure out how to engage your students in unique ways, not to mention being able to incorporate the subjects they're learning about outside your classroom into the novels you're teaching.

A few more things before we start:

- You will notice that in many activities I'll say to "form pairs" or "get into groups of three." Interpret this how you wish. **Every classroom looks different, and you know your students best.** I will say, however, that these activities work best when organized quickly. If they can turn to the person next to them or quickly form groups of three, that will be best. Save the thoughtful partner placements for when you restructure your room or are putting the kids together for formal assessments.

- These lessons are 100-percent adaptable. For example, if I have said to "give an open-ended prompt," and you know that your kids will look at you like you have just spoken to them in Japanese, then *don't do that*. **Adjust and be flexible, as all good teachers do.**

The Tireless Teacher Mini Lessons

1. DIALOGUE TAGS

YOU'LL NEED:
- pen/pencil
- paper

DIFFICULTY:
- easy peasy

Dialogue tags—those little qualifiers at the end of a line of dialogue such as "he said," "she shouted," "they chanted angrily"—are a great way to get kids thinking about how important dialogue is in storytelling. Explain to your students what dialogue tags are, and then brainstorm a list of great dialogue tags together. A list of at least fifteen would be great.

Once you have your list compiled, have students work either independently or in pairs to come up with a story using only dialogue and only the dialogue tags you've brainstormed on the board. You should time this activity at ten minutes, tops. If you have a few minutes to spare before the bell rings, have a few students read their stories aloud.

2. OBJECT OF MY AFFECTION

YOU'LL NEED:
- a bag of trinkets, one for each student
- or one for each group of two (at most)
- pen/pencil
- paper

DIFFICULTY:
- easy and fun!

This is a creative writing exercise that never gets old. It's also fantastic because it can work with seven-year-olds all the way up to seventy-year-olds!

Take out your bag of trinkets and pass them around. When everyone or every pair has an object, tell them this object is extremely special to them. In fact, it's an object that they love. Or maybe has changed their life in some way. Or maybe caused great destruction. Or maybe brought about world peace.

Have students figure out the "why" for their object and then write a story about it. These are tons of fun to share aloud and give your students practice speaking.

3. MEET MY PHILOSOPHER

YOU'LL NEED:
- your stack of philosophers from your toolkit
- access to smartphones
- pen/pencil
- paper

DIFFICULTY:
- moderate

Take out your stack of philosophers and pass them out to your class. If you don't have enough for everyone, have people work in teams of two to three. Then have kids take out their phones (yes, their phones) and research their philosopher.

Write the phrase "Life is" on the board, and tell your class that they are to finish that sentence for their philosopher, based on what they learn in their research. If there is time, have students either present their sentences to the class or present to another person or team.

Depending on your students' interaction with this activity, you might want to extend it into a longer lesson or relate it to a topic you're currently studying.

4. READ THIS!

YOU'LL NEED:

- a paperback book from your shelf for each student

DIFFICULTY:

- easy, if you have a gregarious group!

Have students grab a copy of a book from your bookshelf. It can be any book, really, but for best results avoid the long anthologies. Give students five to ten minutes to read the back cover copy of the book and the first couple of pages, telling them that their job is to now "sell" that book to the person next to them.

If you have time, choose a few students who are really into the "salesperson" roleplay to model for the class! With any luck, you'll have a few students go home with a book to read for pleasure.

Note: you could always have students write down their sales pitch, but I like the idea of having an activity that is just focused on speaking for once.

5. REWRITE IN A NEW PERSPECTIVE

YOU'LL NEED:
- newspaper articles from your toolkit
- pen/pencil
- paper

DIFFICULTY:
- medium, but varies depending on how in-depth you expect your students to go and the difficulty of the newspaper articles you've collected

Pass out some of the articles you've collected in your toolkit and have students read them quietly. These should be short articles, and reading them shouldn't take much time at all. Then, have them rewrite the article from the perspective of another person. It could be silly or serious; it doesn't really matter. What matters is getting kids thinking about how a change of perspective dramatically alters how a story is told.

Note: This is an awesome lesson that could be used to teach about bias! If you want to develop this lesson further, visit www.pbs.org/newshour/extra/lessons-plans/decoding-media-bias-lesson-plan.

6. LET ME BREAK THIS POEM DOWN FOR YOU

YOU'LL NEED:
- poems from your toolkit
- pen/pencil
- paper

DIFFICULTY:
- medium to challenging, depending on the poems you have in your toolkit

We all know that teaching poetry can be a serious challenge, but I think that when kids are given free rein in terms of how they interpret a poem (meaning there are no wrong answers), it can be really fun.

This activity works best in teams. Pass out a poem to each team and tell them that they are now literary scholars being paid an exorbitant (vocab word!) amount of money to explain a poem to a group of college professors. You can have each team start a written speech beginning with, "Dear Distinguished Alumni, let me break this poem down for you." The possibilities for sharing this activity are endless, and it just might get some of your kids interested in poetry.

7. STORY ROUNDS

YOU'LL NEED:
- pen/pencil
- paper

DIFFICULTY:
- easy peasy

This is one of my favorite activities to do to introduce a creative writing unit. Have students take out a blank piece of paper and clear their desk of anything else. Then write on the board a provocative first sentence of a great story. "It was a dark and stormy night" is always a good one. Tell students they have exactly two minutes to continue that story. Don't give them any more information than that—just start timing.

After the two minutes are up, tell them to pass their paper to the person sitting beside or behind them. Everyone should have someone else's paper in front of them. They should read what is already on the paper, and then they have two more minutes to continue *that* story.

This activity can get really silly, and that's okay. If you have more time, you can add prompts like, "Now add the conflict," or, "Now create a resolution to the story in front of you."

8. OSCAR PERFORMANCES

YOU'LL NEED:

- monologues from your toolkit

DIFFICULTY:

- For some kids, this will be easy. For others, super challenging. The trick is to keep it as lighthearted as you can, to take the pressure off the kids who might feel intimidated by public speaking.

This is a great activity for when you are doing a unit in which students will have to speak publicly as part of their assessment. Pass out the monologues from your toolkit in random order. Tell students they have five minutes to read their monologue and become the Meryl Streep they were always destined to be. I would encourage students to share their monologues with the people around them and get ideas during this time.

Depending on the size of your class, you can have one or more students present their monologue, either in front of the whole class or in small groups. This should get loud and dramatic!

9. NEIGHBOR INTERVIEW

YOU'LL NEED:
- pen/pencil
- paper

DIFFICULTY:
- easy to medium

I love bringing journalism into the classroom whenever possible, and this is a great activity to get kids thinking about interview skills. Begin by brainstorming with the class some possible interview questions, including but going beyond silly things like, "What's your favorite color?" Get a great list of questions on the board that will incite thoughtful discussion.

Have students pick a partner (or partner them up yourself) and have them take turns interviewing each other. Tell them to pick three (or more, depending on time) questions from the board and record their answers.

This activity can easily be turned into a longer assignment! Students can present each other to the class or even create a "Meet the Student" interview for a fictional newspaper.

10. THE 15-MINUTE BUSINESS LETTER

YOU'LL NEED:
- pen/pencil
- paper

DIFFICULTY:
- easy, with direction from you

The ability to write a business letter is an important skill that we often don't teach. Go to the board and draw a large rectangle, vertical, like a large piece of paper. See if students can identify the "anatomy" of a business letter, based on what they have seen before. If they can, great! If not, drop some knowledge.

Then, have them write a business letter. They can do this creatively; you'll want to give a prompt to kids who struggle with this. A letter to the superintendent is always a fun one. Have students describe something they like or dislike about school. Or they could write a letter to a politician.

Note: If this fifteen-minute lesson turns into an epic fail, plan to do it again but with more time and structure. This skill is super important, and you don't want to miss your chance to teach it.

11. THE 15-MINUTE EMAIL

YOU'LL NEED:
- pen/pencil
- paper
- (or this can be done on student computers)

DIFFICULTY:
- easy, in theory ;)

If it were up to me, I'd have a full class period devoted to teaching students how to email. Not to click letters and then "send," but to actually write a coherent, clear, respectful, and appropriate email.

Have students compose an email to you, their teacher, letting you know that they will be missing class tomorrow. Don't give them more of a prompt than that.

Take turns reading some of the emails aloud to the class. Chances are, you'll get some really disastrous emails. This should be a lighthearted activity but is actually a great way to show students how communication via email should be taken seriously.

Bonus: have students send their emails to you so you can keep them in your toolkit to revise another time when you're having an "Oh sh*t" moment.

12. THE 15-MINUTE PERSUASIVE LETTER

YOU'LL NEED:
- pen/pencil
- paper

DIFFICULTY:
- medium

We simply don't talk enough about persuasion and how much we are impacted by it every day. I recommend having at least a week in your yearly plans to go over examples of persuasive speeches and elements of persuasion. But for a fifteen-minute activity, have students pull out a blank piece of paper and label it as though it were a business letter. (If you haven't already done the business letter activity, your students will need instructions on how to do this.)

Brainstorm a few scenarios on the board where students would need to persuade someone to do something. Borrowing money from a parent is a good one. Or they might want to persuade their teacher to change a grade, or the principal to extend lunch or recess.

Then, have them freewrite the letter. Tell them they should come up with three good, separate reasons the person should give them what they want. These are fun to read aloud and have students judge whether or not the letter was persuasive enough.

Bonus: you can keep these in your toolkit to revisit/revise another time when you're having another "Oh sh*t" moment.

13. CHANGE MY VIEW

YOU'LL NEED:

- Nothing!

DIFFICULTY:

- Medium to fairly difficult. You'll want your class to be mature enough to handle this one.

If you're familiar with Reddit, you might know of a forum there called "Change My View." It's a place where people post a certain view they feel strongly about (affirmative action, for example) and invite people to politely and respectfully change their view. The idea is that the poster is open-minded enough to receive feedback and debate their viewpoint with the possibility of changing their mind.

Have students work in pairs to come up with something they feel strongly about. This can be as simple as "schools should be able to sell soda on campus" or something much more controversial. You can also assign views to students who are struggling and have them simply pretend they feel that way.

Have those pairs meet up with other pairs. No need for pen and paper with this one—just have the students take turns presenting their views and coming up with different ways of looking at the situation.

14. FOUND POETRY

YOU'LL NEED:
- poems from your toolkit
- paper
- pen/pencil

DIFFICULTY:
- depends on the difficulty of poems in your toolkit

This is a great way to use some of those poems you have collected. Pass a poem out to each student in the class. Make a big show of shuffling them before passing them out so that students know they're getting their poem at random.

Because this activity can get silly, I prefer to have students do this individually. Have them read their poem and try to decipher its meaning. Will you have hands in the air and complaints that they "don't get it"? Yes. Tell them to keep trying, to figure out what at least *part* of the poem is trying to say.

Found poetry is basically a poem made from another text. Once the student has figured out a meaning that makes sense to them, have them rewrite the poem using only the words in the original.

If you have time, have students share their found poems with each other.

15. THE STORY BEHIND THE STORY

YOU'LL NEED:
- newspaper articles from your toolkit
- pen/pencil (optional)
- paper (optional)

DIFFICULTY:
- medium

Take some of those newspaper articles you've collected and pass them out to students in pairs. Tell the students to read the articles as though they are lawyers looking for possible holes in the story. This is a great way for students to practice asking probing questions and looking for motives behind the media articles they read.

Their responsibility is to come up with three "elements" of the story that are missing. Maybe it's the point of view of another person, maybe it's something historical, maybe it's an unanswered question that the writer simply didn't ask but which deserves asking.

If you have time, students can take turns sharing their article and questions with each other or with the class as a whole.

16. LET'S REVIEW

YOU'LL NEED:

- the novel or textbook you are teaching from
- pen/pencil
- paper

DIFFICULTY:

- medium

This is a great activity to do when you're hoping to review a book as a class before a big exam. Break students into groups of no more than three students and assign them either one chapter, a few pages, or one section of the textbook.

Tell them that their group is to summarize that chapter in ten bullet points. No more, no less. Ten bullet points. This will (hopefully) take no more than five to ten minutes.

If you have time, you can have each group present, starting from the beginning of the book. If you don't have time, simply collect the papers and display them around the classroom for a quick all-class review right before the exam.

17. A QUICK EPISTOLARY STORY

YOU'LL NEED:

- pen/pencil
- paper

DIFFICULTY:

- easy peasy

This is a really fun activity to do with a group of creative kids. First, explain that an epistolary story is a story told in letters between people. Then, give students a prompt. Keep it very simple. A love story. A story of loss. A story of revenge. Something like that.

Then, have them begin writing. They can choose the situation, the point of view, and the message in the letter. Give them a time limit—five minutes is plenty.

Finally, have them give their letter to the person next to them. That person should read the letter, assume the role of the person whom the letter has been addressed to, and respond.

Share, if you have time!

18. CULTURAL LITERACY ROUNDS

YOU'LL NEED:
- access to smartphones
- notecards from your toolkit with idiomatic phrases

DIFFICULTY:
- easy peasy

When I taught high school seniors, I always saved a day or two toward the end of the year to talk about cultural literacy. Pass out those notecards from your toolkit with idiomatic phrases; then have kids pull out their cell phones, figure out what they mean, and use them in a unique sentence that showcases the meaning. (Will they copy a sentence from the internet? Probably. Don't worry about it—the point is for them to know what the phrase means and teach it to the class.)

Then, break your class into large groups (you could also do this as one group) and have students explain what each of their idiomatic phrases means. You'll be amazed at how many times you hear random idiomatic phrases being used correctly after this activity.

Note: There are countless ways this activity can be made into a longer, more specific lesson plan. Regardless of what you do with this lesson, I highly recommend having someone write down the idiomatic phrases as you learn and keep them either on a side wall or on a piece of poster paper for the remainder of the school year. Use them often, and help them become part of the conversation in your classroom. That's how they'll stick!

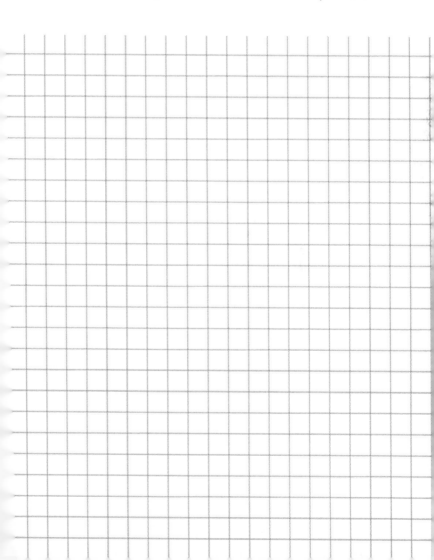

19. A SUPER SILLY IMPROV GAME

FOR HIGH-STRESS DAYS

YOU'LL NEED:

- nothing!

DIFFICULTY:

- easy

In my mind, improv actors are some of the most courageous, talented people on earth. It's one thing to act, but another to do it on the fly. Improv is so much fun too! This is the type of activity you would do to release some tension in the class after a tough day of testing.

Bring two students to the front of the room and tell them to think of a word. Any word. (As long as it's clean, obviously.) Don't have them tell anyone the word. Then, have the students face each other at the front of the room.

You, as the teacher, count to three. On the count of three, they are to say the word to each other *at the exact same time.*

Then, quickly, they do it again. However, this time, tell them to pick a new word based on what they think the person opposite them will pick. The object is to try to get both people to say the same word at the same time.

You keep going a few rounds until they say the same word at the same time or time is up.

Let's be honest—this game is silly and ridiculous. But it's fun! And a great stress reliever after a long day.

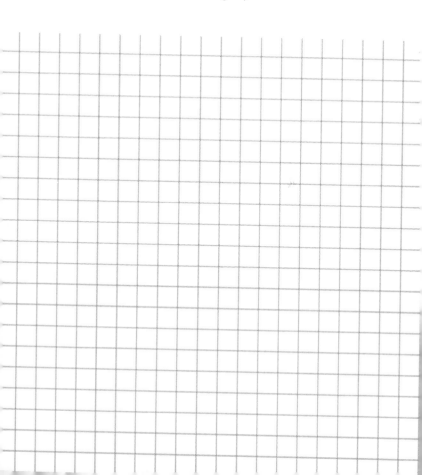

20. REWRITE A SCENE

YOU'LL NEED:

- a class set of either a full play or scenes from a play
- pen/pencil
- paper
- (or this can be done on student computers)

DIFFICULTY:

- medium

This is a great activity to get kids introduced to plays or thinking about how they are structured. If you are in the middle of teaching a unit that revolves around a play, this is a perfect activity to throw in. If not, you can use scenes pulled from any of the plays or monologue books in your toolkit.

I think this activity works best in pairs. Have kids read the scene and then alter some part of it. Maybe it's setting, maybe it's timeline, maybe it's adding an additional character. Maybe they swap characters in the story. Either way, the idea is simple—rewrite the scene with a new element and see how it changes the meaning.

Note: You certainly can have students rewrite scenes on paper or on their laptops, but you don't have to. This also works as a quick conversation around the classroom, either in pairs or as a large group.

21. LEARN THIS SAT WORD

YOU'LL NEED:

- dictionaries from your toolkit
- pen/pencil (optional)
- paper (optional)

DIFFICULTY:

- easy

This is one of my favorite "Oh sh*t" activities. Pass out your dictionaries and have each student pick a word that is new to them. You can put parameters around the words they can pick, but it's not necessary. Tell the students to memorize the definition and use it in a sentence.

Then, have them turn to the person behind them and teach them that word. This is the type of activity that can be done many times in a fifteen-minute period. Who knows—maybe some of the words will stick!

Note: This is another one of those activities that would lend itself to creating a list that will remain hanging in the classroom, either on a piece of paper or on a side board you don't use. Refer to your vocabulary words often, and help them stick!

22. THE MISSING PIECE OF THIS

NEWSPAPER ARTICLE

YOU'LL NEED:
- newspaper articles from your toolkit
- pen/pencil
- paper

DIFFICULTY:
- easy to medium, depending on your news articles

If you have a group of amateur sleuths or kids who are really into deduction, this is a super-fun activity. Pass out newspaper articles from your toolkit to groups of two. Have them read the article with the intent of coming up with questions that they think the article leaves unanswered. Give them a goal of five to ten questions.

This activity isn't great for group sharing. It can move quickly or slowly, depending on the articles you pass out. When groups are done analyzing one article, I would suggest simply giving them another one until the bell rings.

23. CONFIRMATION BIAS

YOU'LL NEED:
- your cell phone hooked up to a speaker (optional)
- a downloaded episode of *Hidden Brain* (optional)

DIFFICULTY:
- this activity is easy, but the resulting conversations (if you choose to have them with your class) can be hard.

This is such an important topic to cover, and you might think it's crazy to do it in a fifteen-minute time span. That would be correct. However, if you think you can make time for two fifteen-minute chunks over the span of a couple of days, or—gasp—a *thirty-minute* chunk of time, you can play the absolutely awesome *Hidden Brain* podcast episode about confirmation bias.

If you don't want to mess with technology, you can read this transcript aloud to the class: www.npr.org/templates/transcript/transcript.php?storyId=519234721

Many episodes of *Hidden Brain* would be great to play in class, but I think this one is a great place to start.

24. 10 TRUISMS

YOU'LL NEED:
- pen/pencil
- paper

DIFFICULTY:
- easy

Define "truism" for the class—something that is obviously true, with no room for debate or question. You can even brainstorm some ideas as a class about things that are "truisms" in their world. (Humans need water to survive. Everything that lives must die.) It is fun to see students struggle to define things that are real, actual truisms.

Then, have students come up with ten truisms about themselves. They have much more leeway, as only they can decide what is actually true for them. This is a fun activity to pair with a philosophy unit, and also a great activity to quickly share with their neighbors. You could also have a ton of fun sharing these, debating some, or saving them to revisit at the end of the school year.

25. SONG LYRICS AS POETRY

YOU'LL NEED:

- access to cell phones
- pen/pencil
- paper

DIFFICULTY:

- easy

If you haven't ever noticed it, songs can either be beautiful or truly terrible poetry. Take away the music and the beat, and it's fun for kids to see if their favorite songs are any good as plain text.

Have them think of their favorite song (be clear that the lyrics must be appropriate) and write down the words on a sheet of paper. They can use their phones if they don't know all the words.

Once everyone has done that, have them analyze the song as though it were a standalone poem. Where would the line breaks be? Is there a rhyme? Is the imagery powerful on its own, or has some of the power been lost as a result of taking away the music?

If there's one popular song that several students choose, it can be fun to play the song for the class and analyze it together, if you have time.

26. PRINCIPAL FOR A DAY

YOU'LL NEED:
- pen/pencil
- paper

DIFFICULTY:
- easy

Tell students they have just been named principal for the day tomorrow, and they need to come up with an agenda for the following school day. This activity can be very formal (business letter) or very casual (vignette). It's really up to you and your students' level.

Here's what is fun about this activity: collect these responses and get them to your school's actual principal! Aside from the obviously silly ones (everyone gets ice cream!) I think it's really valuable to let your principals know what the students are thinking and feeling. I often get very thoughtful responses in this exercise!

27. WHAT'S IN A NAME?

YOU'LL NEED:
- access to cell phones
- pen/pencil
- paper

DIFFICULTY:
- easy

Diving into the meanings behind names is fun for kids of all age levels. Again, this is an activity that can easily be adapted.

Have students write their first name on the top of a piece of paper, along with its meaning. (If they don't know—and many don't—allow them to look it up on their phones. It's usually a quick and easy search.)

Once they know the meaning, have them freewrite about whether or not they think their name truly matches their personality. For some classes, this will turn into a long reflection. For others, they will write one or two sentences. For an added activity, give them the prompt that they must change their name. What would they choose, and why? This can be a really eye-opening activity for kids and can help them get to know each other better.

28. ETYMOLOGY

YOU'LL NEED:
- access to cell phones
- pen/pencil
- paper

DIFFICULTY:
- The hardest part of this is coming up with the words. You can definitely use vocabulary words you've already come up with for this one, or have students go through the novel you're currently reading and come up with a list if it's hard for them to brainstorm words with you.

Define etymology on the board: the study of the origin of words. Then, come up with a list of words as a class that you'd be curious to know the origin of. (Or come up with three or four words for them.)

The activity can simply be the gathering of words—students can research the etymology of them on their own or at another time. You could also have kids present the etymology of different phrases and words in small or large groups. This is another activity that can be done any multitude of ways. Feel free to adapt this idea in any way to fit your classroom.

29. PHILOSOPHIES

YOU'LL NEED:
- access to cell phones
- pen/pencil
- paper

DIFFICULTY:
- easy to medium

Philosophy is one of those subjects that we always want to make time for in class and never do. Because fifteen minutes is hardly enough time to go through all the major world philosophies, anything you can do to whet your students' appetites is great.

Have students pull out their phones and rattle off a numbered list of philosophies. Nihilism, Existentialism, Humanism, Theism . . . the list goes on. See if you can make a list for the exact number of students in your room.

Then, simply assign each student a number. It is their job to define the corresponding philosophy and finish the following sentence: "I believe school is _____" from the perspective of that philosophy.

30. TABOO WORDS

YOU'LL NEED:
- pen/pencil
- paper

DIFFICULTY:
- easy

Inspired by the board game Taboo, this is one of my favorite creative writing warm-ups. Have students think of their favorite food. Then ask them to think of as many words as possible to describe that food. You'll want to make a list of about ten on the board. The more general, the better.

Then, tell students that the key to great writing is to describe things in an interesting and new way. The words they've come up with are the first ones that came to mind, which probably means they are overused.

Have students create a letter (to anyone!) describing their favorite food, but they cannot use any of the "taboo" words on the board. These are really fun to read aloud, if you have time.

31. POETRY BREAKDOWN

YOU'LL NEED:

- One copy of the same poem. Use one from your toolkit that you've made a class set of, or project a poem onto your screen.

DIFFICULTY:

- easy

Break the class into the smallest groups possible. (I think that working individually is best, if possible. While I am a strong proponent of group work and engaging students in all activities, I think it's sometimes very beneficial for students to see their teachers go through the steps of analysis without any expectations of engagement.)

Tell the students that they are to read along with you and watch you analyze. Read the poem in its entirety first and make a statement about it. Then point out any poetic devices you see being used and any specific imagery.

Do not have this rehearsed. They should see you asking questions and being uncertain. That is what analysis is all about! Show them that the process can be fun and interesting.

32. MOTIF

YOU'LL NEED:

- postcards or art from your toolkit (one for each student)
- pen/pencil
- paper

DIFFICULTY:

- medium

Motif is one of those literary devices that lots of kids have heard of but don't quite know what it means. For this activity, pass out copies of either the postcards or the various art cutouts you have in your toolkit. This can be done in groups or pairs but probably works best individually.

Write down the definition of the word "motif" on the board: a distinctive feature or dominant idea. Then, have students figure out the motif(s) in the image before them.

If this is super quick for them or if you have a particularly artistic group, have them sketch a different piece of art with the same motif. If you choose to make this a longer activity, you could hang your works of art around the classroom.

33. ASK ME (ALMOST) ANYTHING

YOU'LL NEED:

- nothing

DIFFICULTY:

- easy

I think that one of the greatest gifts we can give our students is the ability to get to know us as people. If you have a few extra minutes, this is a great activity to do just that.

Think of something about yourself that your students might be interested in. Maybe a career you had before teaching, maybe the city where you grew up, or maybe a friend you have made who is very different from you. Then, in pairs, have them create a question to ask you about that. Often, this is plenty for a fifteen-minute Q and A session.

If this goes very well for you, this is a great activity to do with other students in the classroom. Let the class get to know and learn from each other through a really relaxed Q and A!

34. SIX-WORD MEMOIRS

YOU'LL NEED:
- pen/pencil
- paper

DIFFICULTY:
- easy

This is an activity I often do at the start of a creative writing workshop. Tell students they have only six words to tell their life story. This is a super-fun activity to get kids thinking about word choice and is also a great way to get to know your students.

There are hashtags devoted to this on Twitter. If you have a couple extra minutes, check out some of the incredible memoirs under #sixwordmemoir or #sixwords. As with all things internet, be careful to censor as needed.

35. WORKING DEFINITIONS: SLANG

YOU'LL NEED:

- nothing

DIFFICULTY:

- easy

Nothing like a classroom full of kids using words you don't understand to make you feel old. This activity is something fun to do when the bell is about to ring and you want your kids to teach *you* for a change.

Create a brainstorm on the board of slang words that kids use to describe something "cool." Or something "not cool." It doesn't matter.

Then, task kids to come up with definitions of these words, like their own personal glossary. This can be done in pairs or alone. You can even use the definitions to start a discussion about how the same word can mean different things to different people!

36. MY DREAM JOB

YOU'LL NEED:

- pen/pencil
- paper

DIFFICULTY:

- seems easy . . . but can prove to be challenging (in a good way)

I love to have kids dream of their futures as part of their time with me. For this activity, have students come up with their "dream job." (Yes, it has to be an actual job, or at least sound like it could be an actual job. Professional napper is not an option.) If they can't think of one, assign a job to them.

Then, have them come up with a ten-step plan to making that dream job come true. Yes, *ten steps*. Not three, not nine. Ten.

As you can imagine, this activity gets kids thinking creatively and pragmatically about how to make their dreams come true. If they are forced to come up with ten steps, they will be forced to break down the "big pieces" (like graduating from college) into specifics.

This is a great activity to do in pairs or individually. It can be a springboard to a million other activities as well, such as a larger research project.

37. CHARACTERIZATION

YOU'LL NEED:

- pen/pencil
- paper

DIFFICULTY:

- easy to medium, depending on how you direct their character choosing

Chances are, you talk about characterization *a lot* in your literature class, but this is something a little different. Instead of taking a character from a book, have students choose someone they know and love. If you don't think that will go over well, have them choose from one of the images you have in your toolkit (or you choose one for the whole class).

Then, have them do some characterization around that person. For example, they might make a list of their physical and emotional attributes, the things they like to do, or the things that make them mad.

This can be a springboard for discussion about creating detailed characters, and it can also be the beginning of a larger creative writing project around that character.

38. IF _____ WERE ALIVE TODAY

YOU'LL NEED:

- pen/pencil
- paper

DIFFICULTY:

- easy

This activity is pretty self-explanatory and is best as freewriting. Let students choose whomever they want—a famous person or someone from their personal lives—who is no longer living and have them pretend that person is alive today. They can write whatever they like, but if they need some help, have them write a story from that person's perspective as though they were walking down the street, taking in all the sights.

Again, this can easily be a springboard for a longer and more structured creative writing piece!

39. TED TALK

YOU'LL NEED:

- nothing

DIFFICULTY:

- easy

TED Talks should be a part of your toolkit. There are so many wonderful presentations, many of which are around fifteen minutes long. Perfect!

If you can show a great TED talk, awesome. But another activity you can do is have students get into pairs and plan out their own TED talk. What are they the experts on? What would they be comfortable talking about for fifteen minutes? Can they come up with fifteen bullet points and a title for their presentation?

Of course, the kids won't be presenting these TED talks . . . unless, of course, you want them to!

40. EXPLAIN LIKE I'M FIVE

YOU'LL NEED:

- nothing

DIFFICULTY:

- easy

If you don't use Reddit, you might not know Explain Like I'm Five, or ELI5. This is a forum where people can post about something that perplexes them and have commenters explain it to them in very simple terms. For example, "ELI5: Why is the sky blue?"

In this activity, brainstorm a few things that perplex your students. Come up with a long list on the board. I always find it pretty easy to get the students started on this—there's plenty I'm curious about!

Then challenge students to explain one or more of these things like they're talking to a five-year-old. This is really fun to do with slang terms as well as more complicated issues. You'll probably want your kids to be able to consult Google for this, and if you have time, allow students to share!

41. "WHAT IF"

YOU'LL NEED:

- newspaper or magazine articles from your toolkit
- pen/pencil (optional)
- paper (optional)

DIFFICULTY:

- easy

I absolutely cannot stand it when kids tell me they "can't think of anything to write about." The "What If" game cures that! This game works best in groups of three or four.

Pass out either a newspaper or magazine article to each group. It doesn't matter which. Have one person read the article aloud so everyone in the group hears the story.

Then tell the students that the way to think creatively is to ask, "What if?" Have them brainstorm fifteen to twenty "What If" ideas from that article. For example, if the article is about the president signing a bill into law, they could say, "What if the vice president decided to speak out against the bill?" These can be realistic or totally ridiculous—it doesn't matter. What matters is that students will be left with fifteen to twenty story ideas they can run with if they want.

42. SENSORY DETAILS

YOU'LL NEED:

- trinkets from your toolkit
- pen/pencil
- paper

DIFFICULTY:

- easy

This is an awesome activity to get students to think creatively in a different way. Start by having students think of a specific item—either an object from your toolkit or something in their backpack. Give them about a minute to freewrite a description of that object.

When they're finished, have them reread their description. Then tell them that their challenge is to use a different sensory detail to describe the same thing. (For most students, their writing is heavily focused on how an object looks. Challenge them to use another detail to describe it!)

You can do this however you want, but it's fun to have five one-minute freewrites, all focused on different senses for descriptions!

43. GAME TIME

YOU'LL NEED:

- your bag of trinkets from your toolbox

DIFFICULTY:

- easy

Quickly put your students into pairs or groups of three and give them one, two, or three objects from your bag of trinkets. Students can pick the objects themselves or you can pick for them—it doesn't matter.

Then, tell the groups they have the remainder of the class period to think of a game to play around these activities. No rules, other than students need to use the trinkets they've been given (they can add whatever they want, including drawing a game board, adding play money, etc.) and there must be a winner.

Depending on the class, this might prompt some serious creativity! If so, allow them more time to create their game and maybe present it to the class at another "Oh sh*t" moment.

44. A LETTER TO MY YOUNGER SELF

YOU'LL NEED:
- pen/pencil
- paper

DIFFICULTY:
- easy

This is a really fun one. Tell students they are to write a letter to their younger self. They can choose just how much younger they are for the letter. If students are struggling to figure out what to write, have them come up with five things they wish they could tell their younger self.

This is an awesome activity to have kids read aloud, either in small groups or in front of the class, but only if they are comfortable doing so. If you have time, you can look up some websites devoted to this and read some examples online. Just google "letter to my younger self" and you'll pull up thousands!

45. A LETTER TO MY OLDER SELF

YOU'LL NEED:
- pen/pencil
- paper

DIFFICULTY:
- easy to medium

Like the previous activity, but also a lot different. For this activity, have students imagine themselves at thirty years old (ancient to them!). In their letter to themselves, encourage them to reference specific goals they had in life and assume they achieved those goals.

If you're willing, this is a fun one to collect to get to know your students better and help understand what motivates them or might get their attention in lessons to come.

46. THE FIRST SONG ON MY PLAYLIST

YOU'LL NEED:

- access to cell phones
- pen/pencil (optional)
- paper (optional)

DIFFICULTY:

- easy

A music playlist can tell a lot about a person, can't it? For this activity, give kids permission to check their devices and see the first song in their music playlist. If they don't have a device, have them choose a song that *would* be the first in their playlist.

Then, have students explain to each other why that song is first. This can be done written or just as a casual conversation between two people who don't know each other well.

This is an awesome icebreaker as well as a wind-down activity after a long test or hard lesson. I think that if one song appears at the top of more than four students' playlists, you should listen to it as a class to decide what the buzz is all about.

47. EMPHASIS ON THE WRONG SYLLABLE

YOU'LL NEED:

- nothing

DIFFICULTY:

- easy

This is a fun game to play with your kids who might be a little hesitant to speak in front of a crowd. It also helps kids to see the importance of using their commas and italics correctly.

Write this sentence on the board: "I didn't say I ate your cookies."

Then, take turns saying the sentence aloud, with an emphasis on each different word. "*I* didn't say I ate your cookies." "I *didn't* say I ate your cookies." Talk about how the sentence changes each time!

And if you have time, kids can make up their own sentences that change with different emphasis.

48. LIGHTS, CAMERA, ACTION

YOU'LL NEED:

- pen/pencil
- paper

DIFFICULTY:

- easy peasy

This activity will require a little more imagination and will be perfect for a group of students who are really into film. Tell them to pretend their life is going to be made into a movie, and the casting begins today. Write the important elements on the board:

TITLE:

MAIN CHARACTER:

PARENTAL FIGURES:

SIBLINGS AND BEST FRIENDS:

COMPOSER OF THEME MUSIC:

SETTING:

This won't take long, but it's a really fun one to share as a large group. If you have time, you could have your students identify a song that's already been written that would work as the "theme song" of their life.

49. THE BUTTERFLY EFFECT

YOU'LL NEED:

- pen/pencil
- paper

DIFFICULTY:

- easy peasy

You might want to identify what the Butterfly Effect is before starting this one. You could pull up a clinical-sounding definition, or you could simplify into your (or my) own words: the smallest act, even the flap of a butterfly's wing, has the potential to change the course of the world.

With only fifteen minutes, have students write down "the event" in their lives that they can pinpoint as changing the course of their lives. It could be something big or something small. Give them some time to freewrite about it.

If you want to expand this into a longer lesson, try debating the Butterfly Effect. Have one half of the class argue that yes, small acts do have the power to change the world, and have the other half argue that it's only large gestures which truly change the course of humanity.

50. SLAM POETRY

YOU'LL NEED:

- Technology: you'll be showing a video to the class. If you
  don't have time to get your computer and overhead mon-
  itor talking to each other, let kids whip out their phones
  for this one.

DIFFICULTY:

- This one is super easy, as long as you have technology at the
  ready. You'll be showing videos from YouTube, so be sure
  that your school doesn't have a firewall set up for YouTube.

If students don't know what slam poetry is, enlighten them.
Slam poetry is poetry that is performed, usually as a contest.
The Youth Speaks Teen Poetry Slam is awesome, and their vid-
eos on YouTube are phenomenal.

All you have to do is press play: www.youthspeaks.org/youth-
speaks-teen-poetry-slam

Note: It will probably be easiest if you find a couple of these
in advance and have them bookmarked so that you know the
material and are able to facilitate a quick discussion after watch-
ing. This is a great activity to do on a rainy day or when your
kids are particularly pooped from testing.

51. CAREERS IN WRITING

YOU'LL NEED:
- web access
- pen/pencil
- paper

DIFFICULTY:
- easy peasy

Okay, so this one is a little self-indulgent on my part, but hear me out. When I was a kid, I always wanted to become a writer. All those "college major tests" we did back in the nineties told me I should be a writer. A writer writes books, right? Like Toni Morrison or Stephen King?

If only I could go back in time and tell my young self that a career in writing could be all sorts of things. Maybe I would have avoided some huge mistakes I made in job happiness if I'd been more diligent and resourceful when it came to opportunities for a career doing what I was good at and what I loved.

Have your students google careers in writing. Have them make a list of all the ways a person who is a good writer can make their career in the writing field.

(Oh, and if you have a group of students who just aren't into writing, that's okay. You can still do this. Have students identify something they are good at. Then make a list of job opportunities that await them in that field.)

This fifteen-minute exercise might be life-changing for your students, and motivational to you, as well!

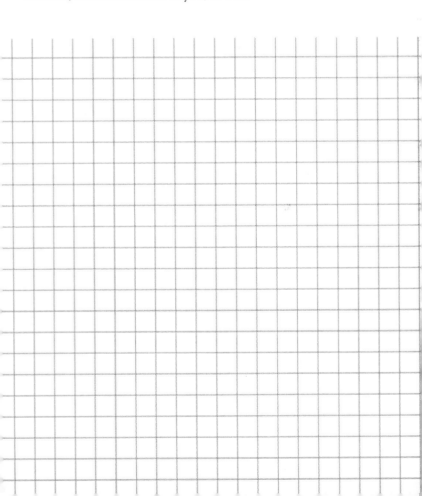

PLACES TO GET TIRELESS TEACHER TOOLKIT ITEMS ON THE CHEAP

1. Freecycle

Freecycle is a website where people post their old crap for free. I am as anti-crap as the next person, but if you have a specific need (such as magazines or newspapers), this might be a great place for you.

2. Public Library Sale Day

I'm sure you know this, but your public library probably hosts two book sales a year. Don't go on the first day, when books can be a whopping one dollar each. Go on the last day, when they're desperate to get rid of inventory. Where I live, the last day of the library sale involves a paper bag, five dollars, and the ability to fill the bag to the very brim.

3. Estate Sales and Garage Sales

Listen, if you have a problem with hoarding junk, then I don't recommend stopping at estate or garage sales (and there are tons of other books that will help you with this problem). But if you need to stock up your toolkit, these events are awesome.

4. Your Parent-Teacher Association

I have a confession to make. In all my years teaching, it never occurred to me to ask the PTA for things if I needed them. But that is what they're there for. If you have a need, the members of your PTA are probably more than willing to help you out—either with collecting some funds or blasting your need for certain items on social media.

5. Your School Librarian or Media Specialist

See if your school librarian or media specialist has any books they are looking to get rid of hidden in corners. You'll be amazed at what they have. Or have lunch with them and see if there are any new resources they know about that they would be willing to share.

6. The Dollar Store

If you don't know what the dollar store is, for the love of all that is holy, get thee to your nearest dollar store! You can easily find pens, paper, and other supplies. If you live in a place without a dollar store, find a friend who does and ask them for a shipment.

7. Facebook

I know, I know. I can hear you through the pages. "I hate social media!" Yeah, me too. It's fine if you don't want to engage on social media. (I totally get it.) But just FYI, Facebook has a "marketplace" where people post things for sale all the time which might be of use to you.

Similarly, I have seen teachers get their needs met through posts on Nextdoor as well. I know, Nextdoor is the worst. But sometimes—sometimes—it's the best.

8. Ask. Directly.

Again, this is something I didn't do enough of when I was in the classroom. If there's a book you really, really want for your classroom and you just don't have the budget for it, ask. Maybe that means asking your room parents. Maybe that means asking another teacher where they got their copy of the book. Maybe that means asking the principal to make a purchase for your department. Maybe that means tweeting an author directly and asking if they'd be willing to donate a copy or two for your education efforts.

The vast majority of people want to help their teachers succeed. So if you need something, don't be too proud to ask.

MY FAVORITE ANTHOLOGIES
FOR MY TIRELESS
TEACHER TOOLKIT

There are several books I couldn't be without in the classroom. Here are a few, with additions from my creative writing classes:

A World of Short Stories by Yvonne Sisko
This is a book of short stories taking place all over the world, complete with comprehension questions and perforated pages. I've gone through several copies of this awesome book.

Good Poems, collected by Garrison Keillor
I love these collections. So much. Great for middle and high school.

The Best American series, various authors
I absolutely love these anthologies, and not just because I can always count on seeing a few copies in my local Goodwill.

There are essays, mystery stories, and some focused on just a specific time period . . . if you ask me, you can't have enough of these books lying around.

Anything by Ann Lamott

Ann Lamott's books are awesome to have at the ready when you have fifteen minutes to read a quick essay and maybe give a dose of inspiration to your class.

Breakfast on Mars by Rebecca Stern and Brad Wolfe

This book of essays is so fantastic that I bought a class set to use for my yearly creative writing workshops. It's a book of essays meant for a young audience about all kinds of topics and all kinds of formats. It's seriously awesome.

What If? by Randall Munroe

Randall Munroe is the creator of *xkcd*, a web comic about science, math, and everything interesting. His website is a really great resource, but this book is a compilation of "what if" questions that are awesome story starters for kids. You'll want this book in your arsenal.

Cultural Literacy: What Every American Needs to Know by E. D. Hirsch Jr.

This book is a treasure for teaching kids idiomatic phrases and is awesome to have on hand to fill in fifteen minutes of your classroom with some fun and relevant information!

The House That Made Me: Writers Reflect on the Places and People that Defined Them by Grant Jarrett

This collection is self-explanatory and a great resource.

Courage: Daring Poems for Gutsy Girls by Karen Finneyfrock

These poems run the gamut of the female experience. A great collection.

Guys Write for Guys Read: Boys' Favorite Authors Write about Being Boys by Jon Scieszka

Awesome, short reflections specific to boys.

Chicken Soup series

Say what you want, but these little books are awesome to have in a pinch. Easy to read and fun to discuss. And they're so ubiquitous that you won't feel bad about cutting them up and using them as handouts during your "Oh sh*t" moments!

FINAL THOUGHTS

Teachers, your job is demanding and often thankless. If you've been teaching forever or you are just starting, knowing (and embracing) those "Oh sh*t" moments doesn't mean you're a bad teacher. It means you're human and always working toward improvement.

Thank you for all you do. Even on the days that are hard. Especially on the days that are hard. We need you.

ACKNOWLEDGMENTS

This book would not have been possible without the support of countless teachers and mentors across two states and two continents who supported me on my own teaching journey. Thank you for giving me tips, tricks, and a friendly ear when I had questions. Thank you for letting me sit in on your lessons and watch you in action. Thank you for telling me it was okay when I messed up and that I would do it better next time. Thank you for believing in me.

Thank you to the staff at Wise Ink Creative Publishing, for all the ways they helped me find my voice as a writer and believed my words mattered.

Special love and thanks to my husband and kids, who let Mommy have writing time because they know it's good for the soul.

ABOUT THE AUTHOR

Roseanne Cheng is a former high school English teacher and author of two young adult books, *The Take Back of Lincoln Junior High* and *Edge the Bare Garden*, which won the gold medal for young adult fiction at the Writer's Digest Self Published Book Awards and the Moonbeam Children's Book Awards. She now works as marketing director at Wise Ink Creative Publishing, where she holds the secondary title of "author therapist" and has the pleasure of helping authors create plans to get their work into the world. She cowrote *Buzz: The Ultimate Guide to Book Marketing* with her dear friend and colleague, Dara Beevas. When she's not reading a book or practicing yoga, you can probably find her hanging out with her hilarious husband of ten years and their two ridiculously awesome kids. Follow her on Twitter @teachablelit.